ALL BUTS STINK!™

HOW TO LIVE YOUR
BEST LIFE *AND*
ELIMINATE EXCUSES

WALTER BOND

ALL BUTS STINK!
How to live your best life
by eliminating the excuses
By Walter Bond

Copyright © 2007 (revised edition)

All Buts Stink! How to Live Your Best Life by Eliminating the Excuses™ is a trademark of Motivation Made Easy Publishing, Motivation Made Easy Publications, Walter Bond Seminars denoting a series of products that may include but is not limited to books, audio products, video products, pocket cards, calendars, T-shirts, coffee mugs and more.

Published by:
Motivation Made Easy Publishing
A subsidiary of Walter Bond Seminars, Inc.
Minneapolis, MN

www.walterbondseminars.com

Printed in the United States of America.
Cover design and layout by Bethany Press, Inc, Bloomington, MN

ISBN: 0-9787805-0-7

TABLE OF CONTENTS

All Buts Stink!

All Buts Stink!

I couldn't resist writing a book that would help people who are motivated to reach their full potential *"but"* need some encouragement and support getting to the next level of excellence. One of the biggest reasons a person is stymied or has become stagnant is because of the unnecessary use of excuses. How many times have you heard someone use the word *"but"* to justify an area in which they haven't had success? "I would be an executive *'but'* my company plays too many political games." "I should have been the one promoted *'but'* I believe ***ALL BUTS STINK!*** Every time you hear someone say the word *"but"* start sniffing because the next few words will be a smelly excuse. Success can be boiled down to a few simple fundamentals. I want to make sure you know these fundamentals and execute them on a daily basis. I wrote this book to take all your excuses away.

When I think about my success in sports and business and all the other successful people who have crossed my path during my lifetime, I am thoroughly convinced there are fundamentals to success that transcend all industries. Sometimes you don't know what you don't know. Right now there are many things you don't know *"but"* you don't know that you don't know them. Therefore,

I want to make sure you know my fundamentals of success and understand how to execute them daily. Stop making excuses; your life is entirely your fault. On every level of basketball I played, our practice was a simple exercise in mastering the fundamentals of basketball. Therefore, in my career as an athlete, basketball practice at the high school level was very similar to my college practice and my pro workouts, as well. What allowed a select few players to become NBA players? The players who were able to reach the pinnacle were those who mastered the fundamentals. The same goes for you. Your success will be based on how well you master the fundamentals of your industry and profession.

What would happen to your life if you mastered the fundamentals of professional success? I have prepared some easy and commonsense approaches for taking control of your life through some steps that can be easily executed. However, if you don't know the fundamentals or fail to execute them, you will never operate at your full potential as an athlete, professional, parent or spouse. What you will learn in this book will be different from most books because I am not covering information I read in some other book. All of the content has been taken from my own personal and real-life experiences, of both my successes and failures in sports and business. This book is from my heart--it is from what I have lived, and my hope is that you will find the content to be fresh, sincere, and life-changing.

Are you ready to learn the fundamentals of success that can transform your life? After you read this book, you will agree with me that *ALL BUTS STINK!* and you will eliminate excuses forever.

Preface

I was born the youngest of four children in the inner city of Chicago to Gloria and the late Willie Bond. They were educators in the Chicago public schools. My dad was the principal at Collins High School on the west side of Chicago and my mom taught kindergarten at Coles Elementary on the south side of the city. Chicago is a hot bed for high school basketball. My dad's school had a very good basketball team and I eventually transferred to his school from Whitney Young High School, which was a wonderful academic institution, *"but"* I left to improve my chances of playing Division I basketball and eventually play in the NBA. My dad was 6'6", 240 pounds, and he ruled the hallways of his high school with an iron fist. This, of course, made my experience there very unique. I didn't live by the school and the students saw me as a spoiled brat from the nice part of town. I was the principal's son and eventually became one of the stars of the basketball team. After a few years and a lot of basketball success, most of the students and teachers eventually accepted me and I became involved in almost everything that happened at the school, on the basketball court, and in the classroom.

I accepted a basketball scholarship to the University of Minnesota and walked on campus as the savior (at least in my mind) of their basketball program and was expecting to receive all the attention and success I had grown accustomed to in Chicago. When the first game started, guess what? My name was not in the starting lineup; in fact, it very seldom was. I was not a starter for my college basketball team and spent most of my time on the bench as a reserve. It was a struggle to keep a good attitude and also to keep my dream alive of playing in the NBA. The smartest thing I did each year was to sit down with the coaches and have them evaluate my season and let me know what I needed to work on for the next season. I did just that for all fours years and was voted most improved player every season I attended the university. The NBA was still a possibility if everything went well my senior season. However, during my senior season I broke my foot twice and my college career was over. I almost accepted a job to become a hospital administrator *"but"* called my dad right before I accepted the job offer and he asked me a simple question. "Do you believe you can play in the NBA, son?" I told him yes. Immediately, he asked me another question. "Why don't you go for it?" " *'But'*, dad, I never started in college, *'but'* dad I only averaged 7 points a game, *'but'* dad, no one in the NBA will give me a chance." *"But"*, *"but"*, *"but"*, I said *"but"* about 30 times in a five-minute conversation. Hence, *ALL BUTS STINK!* was born. My father eventually convinced me to go for it by asking the right question. I improved so much that I was given a tryout with the Dallas Mavericks a year after I left college and polished my skills in the minor league called the CBA in Wichita Falls, Texas. When I went to training camp, I was so ready and so focused and on this track of continuous improvement that not only did I make the team, I became a starter and was the first rookie free agent to ever start opening night for the Dallas Mavericks. I went on to have an eight-year career in professional basketball playing for the Dallas Mavericks, Utah Jazz, and Detroit Pistons. I also played in Greece, Italy, and Germany and finally closed the basketball chapter of my life with a stint as a broadcaster for the Minnesota Timberwolves. I don't know what kind of *"buts"* you have in your life, *"but"* I do know this--they all stink.

Is there any benefit to a bad attitude? If so, please let me know.

— *Walter Bond*

CHAPTER ONE

Your Attitude Is Your Fault

By definition, attitude is a state of mind or a feeling, or disposition. Do you have a handle on your attitude? How do you respond, react, and perceive situations and circumstances? Do you know that your attitude is the most crucial factor in how high you will excel in life? Good attitude—good life; great attitude—great life; bad attitude—bad life. We have all heard the saying, "Your attitude will determine your altitude." What a true statement. Before I introduce the keys to a good attitude, let me ask you a question. Is there any benefit in having a bad attitude? No, there is not one positive benefit to a bad attitude. I sure can't think of one, can you? We all have an attitude and it is transmitted by our presence. In some cases you can tell a person's attitude without them even opening their mouth.

Attitude separates good individuals from great individuals, average producers from great producers, good companies from great companies, good families from great families. Your overall success in life is based on your ATTITUDE!!! There have been countless examples of famous and ordinary people who have experienced struggles *"but"* because of their attitude they went on to do even greater things. Do you believe that *"but"* is a huge part of their vocabulary? No!! Of course not! I am sure they agree that ***ALL BUTS STINK!***

Abraham Lincoln, a legend in American history, failed so many times we lost count. In fact, before being elected President, he had a nervous breakdown. However, his attitude allowed him to persevere and become a pioneer in so many ways for our country. There are countless examples of famous people who persevered and became triumphant because of their attitude. I won't bore you with them all. Just remember this, your attitude will make or break your career. There is no excuse not to have a good attitude. "***But***' if you only knew my wife or my husband or my boss…" Remember ***ALL BUTS STINK!*** No more excuses! Here are four keys that can help you have a good attitude.

I. Make the most of every situation.

When we have a good attitude we can make the most out of every situation. Often, it appears as if life brings us challenges just to see what we are made of. If everything were always perfect in your life, how would you know the extent of your character? Life's challenges have a way of bringing out the best or worst in you, *"but"* either way at least you are out. The perfect time to make lemonade is when you have been given lemons. Always make the most of every situation that comes your way. For example, don't complain that the hotel is too far away from the parking lot, take this as an opportunity for a much needed workout. Don't complain about the traffic jam because I know people who value that time as a way to debrief the day before they go home to their family. Don't complain about the rain outside, just think about how much your yard needs it or the farmer who lives off the land and needs the rain to survive. Become a person of positive action, be quick on your feet and be ready to respond the right way any time you are faced with a less than perfect situation. On your next delayed flight, instead of venting to airline employees, baggage handlers or anyone that will listen, use this time as an opportunity to catch up on some much needed paperwork or perhaps finish the book you've been reading. You can always make the most out of every situation.

Train your mind to think about life as a game, where the best attitude always wins. Turn life into this game and you will always win. Every situation, every encounter, every job, every opportunity, every loss--make the most out of it. You must look at everything that comes your way as a test to see how you can make the most out of it. Pass the *"make the most of it"* test every time you take it. Always pass the test.

II. Discipline your mind.

The second key is disciplining your mind. Our thought processes can be so undisciplined. Your mind is the most powerful part of your body and you must respect it. You are a prisoner of your thought life. How you think will dictate your attitude, how you think will drive your behavior. How do you know if your thought life is healthy? How disciplined is your mouth? Do you listen to what you are saying? Do you ever hear yourself speak and say yuck? If you say "yuck," how often do the people around you say "yuck?" If you are honest with yourself, there are situations in which you do not speak the right things. We will speak exactly what we think, believe it or not, we all think before we speak. If you find yourself saying the wrong things it's only because you've been thinking the wrong things. We can think the wrong things and say the wrong things. We can think the right things and say the right things, *"but"* we can't think the right things and say the wrong things. That is absolutely impossible to do. Control your mind, control your mouth and control your life. It is amazing what people can say out of their mouths and then wonder why things don't work out. If a wife says every day, "I have a terrible marriage, my husband is a jerk." Guess what kind of marriage she is going to have? Why? She will focus on exactly what she says. Don't you think this will affect how she views her husband and marriage? She will focus on every negative attribute or flaw and ignore the positive attributes of her spouse all together. You can sabotage your life with your own mouth.

I have made a commitment to ask people how they are thinking rather than asking how they are doing, because how they are thinking will affect how they are doing. Make sense? Control every thought that comes into your head and think the best of every person, situation, or experience. Always, look at the bright side. You may think you were born too fat, too skinny, too short, too tall, too rich, or too poor. Wait a minute!!!! What are you focusing on? I believe 90% of your life is good, that leaves 10% that is less than perfect. Hey! You may have 10% of your life that is awful. However, what percent you decide to focus on is critical. Do you focus on the 90% or the 10%? Train yourself to focus on the 90%, and when you find your mind drifting toward the 10%, stop yourself and focus back on the 90%. I am not suggesting you ignore the 10%, you will think about it and you should do what you can to improve it. All I am recommending is to not let what's wrong with your life consume your thought process and drown out the 90% that is good. Discipline your mind to meditate on the good things in your life and your attitude will correspond.

III. Be selfless.

The third key to maintaining a good attitude is to be selfless. The happiest people you want to meet are the selfless ones. It doesn't matter how much money they make, selfless people are always happy people. Believe it or not, there are people whom actually take joy in helping their fellow men and are not consumed with themselves. Selfless people are a dying breed, almost extinct...instead of focusing on saving dying breeds such as; pandas, eagles and emus--we should try to repopulate this earth with more selfless people. Have you ever been around someone who is too self-involved? They will wear you out when you speak to them. These people are so self involved it makes you so sick you want to puke right over the phone. They can drain the very life from you because all they want to do is to talk about themselves, their lives and always have something to complain about. These kinds of people are draining and will always have issues until they take the focus off themselves. You mark my words, these people are **never** happy with life. Something is always wrong. Why? We don't function best as humans when we focus on ourselves, we implode. It is amazing that we all want to be kings and queens *"but"* it's the servants who are often the happiest. Why is that? When you are consumed with yourself you can never get enough. You can never get enough money, power, fame, fortune, or credit--if that is what makes you happy. You can never be happy because no matter how much you have, you need a little bit more. The more you get the more you want and you turn into a monster with an unrelenting appetite. Isn't that at the core of our recent corporate scandals?

I don't think any of us can have a true impact in society until we get over ourselves. When I say get over yourself, I mean to take the focus off you. This is a process, *"but"* it should be a quest for all of us to do as quickly as we can because our happiness and attitude depends on it. If a person is selfish and self-serving, they will often have a bad attitude. A selfish person is only concerned about how something affects them. When things are working out well for them they are happy campers. However, when they get the short end of the stick, here comes trouble, here comes the attitude. The attitude is never too far away. If you know anyone who is moody or inconsistent with their attitude, the root of it is always selfishness. Why do you do what you do? How does it affect those around you? Does it only benefit you? When I find myself having a struggle with my attitude, I check myself to see if I am being selfish or selfless, and then try to discover why. Usually when my attitude is going sour, I remind myself to focus my attention on helping someone else and take my eyes off me.

Do you know any selfless people? I am sure you know people who are generally concerned about the welfare of others. When you have time make a list of the most helpful people you know and do a quick case study of their attitude. Aren't they happier people on average? I have seen people who are dirt poor *"but"* are happy people because there is an element of emotional prosperity when you help someone else. It profits us tremendously when we take the focus off ourselves and put it on others. Being selfless is a powerful way to manage your attitude.

Don't blame outside forces!!!! Outside forces give us the chance to respond appropriately based on what we possess on the inside. The check-out lady being rude to you at the grocery store is no excuse for you to be rude. She didn't make you act rude, you made a decision to be rude. A selfless person, with a disciplined thought process, won't lash back *"but"* will focus on the check-out lady. The thoughts might be, "she must be having a bad day," "poor soul, maybe she is stressed out." If you are selfish, you will focus on how they made you feel and lash back. If you are selfless, you will take it on the chin or better yet offer a word of encouragement. Your attitude will always drive your behavior. Be selfless. It's refreshing and it helps to get the focus off you. You have already done enough thinking about yourself for a lifetime. Please get over yourself so you can be the great resource that you really are.

IV. Have short-term memory.

The fourth way to maintain a good attitude is by having short-term memory. Why should Monday affect Tuesday? It shouldn't. Every day is a new day. It's easy to fall into the trap of holding onto wrong thoughts from one day to the next, even longer. Have short-term memory when it comes to negative experiences and hold onto the positive ones. You will become what you meditate on, so mediate on the good things that happened to you today and let the bad ones go. What do you do if someone mistreats you? It is okay to have a conversation with your spouse or loved one to reconcile in your mind what happened, then release it. Once you release it, it is gone, replace it with good thoughts of that person. Out of sight is out of mind. If you don't focus on the negative you will forget about it very soon. Again, this is a mental discipline that is actually very fun to practice. We all have experienced times when we let our minds go unchecked and find ourselves thinking negative thoughts about people or situations. Your attitude will greatly benefit from short-term memory on negative thoughts *"but"* it will also benefit by meditating on the positive things that happened during the day. Then watch what happens to your attitude. If you are not careful you can let an event that took place in your childhood afflict you for years. If you meditate on the good things in life, the bad things will lose their grip on your mind and ultimately your attitude. Every night empty out your mind of the negative and horrible things you heard, said or did throughout the day so you can start fresh anew the next day.

Make the most out of every situation, discipline your thought life, be selfless and have short-term memory. Your attitude will drive your behavior. Please, stay mindful of all the components I have shared in this chapter. You will be unstoppable, because no one can stop you *"but"* you. There is no benefit to a bad attitude, so why have one. *"'But'* Walter you don't understand my situation." Maybe I don't, *"but"* I do understand *ALL BUTS STINK!*

CHAPTER TWO

Dominate Right Where You Are!

If your desire is to reach the pinnacle in your industry, you must know how to get there. I want you to know how to get there. You need a road map. Everyone wants to get to the next level, some more than others, *"but"* few know how to get there. The key to your promotion is your current situation. Why do you feel entitled to more if you haven't maximized what you already have? Wherever your life is right now the key for you to reach the next level of success is to dominate right now, right where you are. You must master your current situation. Stop complaining! Stop moaning! Stop grumbling! Dominate right where you are and the next level for you is right around the corner.

So, let me guess? You think you are overqualified for your current position with your company. I hope you think this way. If you don't, I think that would be an even bigger problem. I am impressed that you have such healthy self-esteem. However, do your peers agree? I know so many people who think they are overqualified for their positions, salaries, and responsibilities, *"but"* they are the only one who thinks so. Your situation won't change until others think the same way about you. Your situation won't change a bit until everyone else agrees that you are in fact overqualified for your position. Get a clue, everyone at your company thinks they are overqualified for their position too; including your CEO. The key to your next promotion or increase in responsibility is to be awesome at the responsibilities you have right now. When you dominate your current circumstances long enough, others will take notice and your promotion and increase will come. You can't be denied *"but"* if I don't get that promotion, I'll quit." As I told you before--*ALL BUTS STINK!* You may need to leave your current company or industry to get what you deserve, *"but"* chances are that your opportunity can happen right where you are, if you dominate.

I remember when I sat on the bench with my college basketball team. I had dreams and aspirations like all my teammates to make the NBA *"but"* I found myself on the bench as a reserve. The odds were slim of making the NBA as a starter in college basketball, *"but"* there was no room for a reserve in college basketball to make it in the NBA. It didn't even sound logical for a reserve to make the NBA. I didn't let that stop me because I know that *ALL BUTS STINK!* I decided to make the most out of my opportunity. Whenever my coach Clem Haskins called on me I would do whatever I could do with the amount of time he gave me, playing whatever role he needed. If he played me one minute I tried to make that one minute memorable. Well, by dominating where I was, my minutes increased and in a few years I was the first rookie free agent to start for the Dallas Mavericks in the NBA.

I took this same attitude into my speaking business. In fact, Clem Haskins is the person that encouraged me to become a motivational speaker. The first time I was paid to speak professionally I received $25 in gift certificates to Applebee's. I dominated that keynote opportunity and every other chance I had, and from that point on in a few short years I doubled my NBA income and was named "Speaker of the Year" in 2005 by *MME*, a meeting planners' publication.

My first big break in the speaking business came when I was booked by a financial service company to present at their national sales meeting. It was an awesome experience for me as a speaker and my first big-time keynote for a corporate client. I actually was able to go out of town, on a plane, and somebody actually paid my full fee for me to speak. Can you imagine that? The client picked me up from the airport in Phoenix in a Lincoln Town car that was jet black with black tinted windows. Then the driver carried my luggage from the baggage claim right to the car and opened and closed my door. He even handed me a bottle of water and a *USA Today* once I buckled up. I felt strange because I was much bigger than he was and I had to watch him struggle with my two large bulky bags, *"but"* he took so much pride in his job I would have insulted him tremendously if I had helped. Wow!!! I felt like a million bucks and I couldn't wait to speak at their event as their closing speaker. I was poised to give them the best keynote they ever had or the best keynote I had ever delivered, which ever applied was fine with me. When we pulled up to the luxury hotel in Phoenix, I noticed at least ten bellboys waiting to carry luggage for hotel guests. I am from Chicago and I know a scam when I see one. These guys will grab my bags before I can and try to make me give them a tip. When the car finally stopped, I ran to the back to beat the bellmen and my driver to my luggage. It almost turned into a polite fight over a tip. We fought and struggled over my luggage for a few seconds, then I politely said, "No, I'm fine.

I'm okay, I don't need any help," as I yanked at my luggage. Finally one of the bellmen perceived what was happening with this rookie guest, and said, "Mr. Bond, the tips are already taken care of." I stopped dead in my tracks, released my bags, and replied, "knock yourself out, dude" I knew then that this was a different place and I couldn't wait to get inside my room to live like a king for the next two days. I rushed up to my room right before the luggage arrived and it was a sight to behold. My room was awesome, the towels were perfect, the blankets and comforter looked like clouds. There were even q-tips and cotton balls in the bathroom and a nice balcony with a gorgeous view of the property.

I knew that this room had to pass one final litmus test-- the bath rob test. I rushed to the closet and there to my delight was one of the most plush, elegant bathrobes I had ever seen. I hadn't stayed in a hotel of this caliber since my NBA days had ended a few years prior. I knew my luggage would show up in a few minutes so I decided to get undressed and throw on my bathrobe. It was wonderful! I pranced around the room as if I was royalty. Then I noticed there was a letter B monogrammed on the lapel. I thought this "B" stood for Bond, of course, and I felt as if I owned the place. Finally, I heard a knock at the door. It was the bellboy with my luggage. I could see him through the peephole in the door. Now these guys were already suspicious of me from my earlier behavior in the parking lot. So the moment he saw me in this bathrobe it was confirmed that I was a very unique and special guest. You see, the bathrobe I had on was only a medium and I am 6'5", 250 pounds. He rushed into the room, dropped my bags, and ran out as though he had seen a ghost. The sleeves were above my elbow and it only draped me slightly below the rib cage. Why did I put it on? I was in a great hotel, that's why! I was so happy,

I didn't complain and I didn't grumble, I just wore the robe I had been given.

Isn't life the same way? People complain all the time about their office, their salary, their body, their spouse, their kids, and their car. You know what? Stop complaining and just wear the robe you've been given. A few minutes later the bell captain returned, (with security, I might add) and said, "Mr. Bond, I couldn't help *'but'* notice the bathrobe you are wearing is too small." I looked down myself and also saw the obvious. He said, "Here is a bathrobe that is just your size." It was an XXL bathrobe. They rushed out before I began to change into my new one. You see, you are probably right. You are overqualified for your position. *"But"* instead of murmuring and complaining about it, start dominating right where you are, and I guarantee you that someone else will notice and bring you a new job, salary, responsibility, and a bathrobe that is just your size. Start dominating the life you've been given and, trust me, others will take notice. *"'But'* my boss is a jerk." *ALL BUT'S STINK!* Your promotion may not come from your boss. Believe me when I say this, people are always watching you everywhere you go. Just dominate right where you are and the laws of nature will make sure your promotion and increase comes. Dominate right where you are, wear the robe you've been given and you will ultimately get exactly what you deserve.

I first learned this lesson playing college basketball at the University of Minnesota. I never started for the team. It was frustrating and made me angry. *"But"* once I got my attitude right I decided to make the most out of my situation. In a matter of a few years, I was known as the best sixth man in the country. Some of my teammates quit mentally when they weren't placed in the starting lineup. They developed bad attitudes and stopped working. Instead, they spent their time complaining rather than getting better. There was a good reason we were all on the bench--we were on the bench because there were five other players who were better than us. However, I never stopped working and believing and I dominated every opportunity I was given. If the coach played me five minutes, I gave it all I had for five minutes. If it was ten minutes, I gave all I had for ten minutes and before I knew it others began to notice and my value increased. A year later I became the first rookie free agent to start opening night for the Dallas Mavericks. I had not started a basketball game since high school, *"but"* here I was playing my first NBA game, wearing a real NBA uniform, in a real NBA arena, with real NBA music and my name announced in the loud speaker. "Starting at shooting guard for your Dallas Mavericks, 6'5", 215 pounds, from Chicago, Illinois, Walterrrrrrrr Bond!!!!!!" You see, by dominating a role I thought I was overqualified for put me in a position for the NBA to notice and they gave me a position, a salary, and responsibility that was just my size. You can experience the very same thing in your life. The key is to dominate wherever you are right now and wear the bathrobe you've been given. Someone will notice--I guarantee it. *"But"*, *"but"*, *"but"* you know the drill--***ALL BUTS STINK!*** Dominate right where you are and your life, career, marriage, and children will become what you dream about.

CHAPTER THREE

Master Information!
Master Discipline!
Master Life!

Master Information!

Here is a profound thought: "People fail because of a lack of information and/or discipline." In fact, I have so much confidence in you that I can confidently say that the only thing that can stop you from constantly growing and increasing your value is to reject new information or have poor discipline executing what you know. You can trace almost every problem you have to a lack of information and/or discipline. This concept is powerful if you can embrace it. If you can get your arms around this one thought, you're well on your way to greatness. You can take total control of your life by simply accessing the right information and living a life of discipline.

With the internet as a part of our culture today, there is absolutely no excuse not to have information available to you on any subject you need. We all can have access to the right information from around the world at the touch of a button. In my opinion, ignorance is a choice--a wrong one that will never pay off. Remember, if you fail to access or reject new information, that is really the only way you can be stopped and you would have done it to yourself. Self-inflicted ignorance is no way to live. If any of your friends, colleagues, or co-workers have stopped growing emotionally, personally, mentally, spiritually and professionally, you can always trace their stagnation to a lack of information and/or a lack of discipline.

One great way to add to your knowledge base is by reading books, newspapers, magazines, attending seminars and conferences. There is so much information available and it is so easy to get your hands on it there is no reason why you shouldn't possess all the information you need to be incredibly successful. I encourage you to decide to ramp up on your reading and your personal quest for new information. I strongly encourage you to start with your industry first and become a premier expert in your industry. Then as you gain confidence with that, expand your reading and read about everything: business, sports, entertainment, politics and world events. Gather information all the time, you can't afford to stop gathering information in life at any time. In life we are in the information-gathering business. If you stop gathering information you will stop maturing and your effectiveness will be capped off. Have you ever met a person who seems immature for their age? There is a very simple reason for this. They stopped gathering new information about life. You can't stop gathering information in any aspect of your life; we need information in every life discipline. You may be doing a good job of gathering new information for your job because you want a promotion, *"but"* doing poorly on gathering more information about becoming a better parent or spouse. I once heard a wise man say, "The more I learn, the more

I realize how much I don't know." When you constantly gather new information, it not only increases your IQ *"but"* it can and will challenge and change your thinking.

You can't increase your influence or value in the marketplace staying exactly the way you are right now. We should all grow and increase in value just like fine wine does over time. This is how I believe we really grow and mature. Our circumstances rarely change; *"but"* what really changes is how we respond to our circumstances. If we gain some new information and respond differently to our circumstances based on that new information, our results will be different. These different responses allow for different results that should begin to form our new life. Nothing frustrates me more than to see a person have a problem, try one solution, have that solution fail; then keep doing the same thing over again the same way, using the same techniques, and still not getting the results they desire. How dumb is that! You must keep trying new ideas, new strategies, and new techniques for whatever area you're working on until you get the results you desire.

The positive result of gathering information is this; you should be able to have an intelligent conversation with everyone you meet on at least three different topics that are important to them. I teach relationship-building techniques in many of my seminars. Relationship building is important in leadership, sales, teambuilding, family, marriage, or whatever you do that involves people. If you can't build relationships, you won't sell anything and you won't lead anything. You may be in charge *"but"* you will never lead. There is so much to talk about in life and you need to possess enough information to keep others engaged.

Another benefit to being in the information-gathering

business is that the more your information increases the more effective you can be in social circles. You need this because people possess a lion share of information you need. How many times has a person you know turned you onto a realtor, a new school, a new restaurant, the right sixth-grade teacher, coach, or neighborhood? Everyone you know has some information on marriage, parenting, fashion, or whatever you need. If you can talk about a multitude of topics you can connect with everyone you meet. The transfer of information is the key to any healthy relationship. This qualifies you to spend more time with them; thus gaining more information both parties desperately needs. The most valuable resource in gathering information is not the internet, books, or seminars, although they are important, *"but"* it is people. People are absolutely amazing.

Become an expert.

The one thing I noticed when I entered the business community from the athletic industry was that many professionals are lazy. There, I said it! I hope I hurt your feelings because it's true. Many beer belly fans go to the local arenas and rip professional or collegiate athletes for anything they feel doesn't live up to their expectations of excellence, *"but"* forget they are watching the best in the world. If you want to become an expert in your industry you must possess more information, expertise, and skill than anyone else. I say it all the time—If you want to be considered an expert in your industry, you should have read a minimum of 100 books on the subject. I have heard other experts say you should read 2500 books about your industry to become an expert. If your industry is hands-on, then get your hands on it. Spend every moment learning more and more about your industry and perfecting your particular expertise. What a great advantage for you if you know more than others know in your industry, in your company, in all your circles. I don't want you to be "a know it all," *"but"* I am talking about being a well-informed expert in your industry and you will be a good conversationalist and others will start to recognize, appreciate and eventually compensate your expertise.

Have you ever had the experience of calling a company to ask a question and the person who answers the phone can't answer your question? *"But"* they put you on hold and consult someone else. Guess what? The person they consulted for the answer is probably more valuable because they possess more information and expertise. In more cases than not, the person who was consulted makes more money.

Your mind is like a parachute, it will open up as wide as you need it, *"but"* it will stay closed if you don't put anything in it. Racism, diabetes, AIDS, poverty, cancer, and other life-threatening illnesses can be avoided by attaining the right information. The right information can save your life. The wrong information can kill you. That should sum up how important information is.

Information can either reinforce what you believe or challenge your thought process. Always be open to new information, no matter how much you know. You don't know it all, so you need new information or run the risk of maintaining and nourishing your ignorance. Do you know that you possess information that can improve or even change a person's life? We all should transfer information with everyone we encounter. Remember, the transfer of information is the key to any healthy relationship. We all should empower, encourage, and strengthen each other in our relationships, business circles, and communities. We are so worried about people spreading AIDS, hepatitis B or the bird flu.

If you are going to be around me, infect me with some of your knowledge. Healthy relationships rely on the transfer of good information. When you possess good information you become a portal for others and your value keeps increasing.

Master Discipline!

Remember my profound thought earlier, *People fail from a lack of information and/or discipline?* The first step is to seek new information. The next step is discipline. This simply means to act on the information you know on a consistent basis. We must be disciplined in our execution in order to reap the benefits of the new information we acquire. For example, we all know people who smoke. I'm sure they all know that smoking can kill you. Do you know second-hand smoke can kill you too? Smoking can cause all sorts of health issues for the smoker and everyone close to them. However, we still have people that know this information *"but"* continue to smoke and put others at risk--people they claim they love. We can possess all the information in the world *"but"* a lack of discipline will hurt us every single time and maybe even kill us and the people around us.

Discipline deals with your belief system. If you believe that a certain activity can produce a certain result, your discipline is based on faith. So when a person has confidence that a certain activity will produce a certain result, executing is no problem. The root word of discipline is **disciple**, which means to be a follower of. So discipline simply means to follow something. So what are you following? The good news about discipline is that you only have to do it one day at a time. If you can master one day of discipline, you can master a week, then a month, and ultimately you can master your life. The key to discipline is taking one day at a time, focusing every day on discipline and you'll see the results very soon. This will give you the energy to stick to your discipline for the long haul. Once you do this for 365 days, the results can be incredible, *"but"* it all starts with being a disciple of a plan based on the information you possess for one day and linking those days together.

How much would a company benefit from disciplined employees who execute the business plan, marketing plan, sales strategy, customer service, or strategic plan? I train sales reps to be disciplined on their complete sales cycle. If they are, they close more sales, build larger client bases, and reap greater returns. How much weight would we all lose if we followed the diet and workout schedule that has been proven to work? Remember, all diets work. It's not the diet that didn't work, you didn't work the diet.

Discipline even works when you don't feel like doing it. Trust me, whatever discipline you enter into, you won't feel like doing it every day. However, do it anyway because it will still have a positive effect. Remember, all problems can be traced back to a lack of information or discipline. Why let a problem exist in your life when the answer can be easily found and executed?

I guarantee that discipline will start to take you places you have never been before. It might be painful in the beginning and tough to execute; *"but"* in the end you will benefit enormously and you will become more productive and successful. I believe that naturally our human nature doesn't desire a plan that controls us *"but"* we all innately know we need discipline. Life is a discipline. Have you ever met a person who is undisciplined have success over a long period of time? You can survive for a while on talent *"but"* I will bet my last dollar on a less talented person or company that is well disciplined than an undisciplined person or company with talent. We can all put our lives on auto pilot if we just remember to follow through on the information we possess and live with discipline. When you possess something, you own it, it's yours. I know two things for sure: if you always access new information and live a disciplined life your value will always increase. "I could gather more information *'but'* I don't have enough time." *ALL BUTS STINK!* What better investment of your time is there than to broaden your knowledge? Master information! Master discipline! Master life!

CHAPTER FOUR

Vision Is As Vision Does

Let's talk about your personal vision. So let's begin by defining what vision is. Vision is how you see the completion of your future in every detail. Vision is how you see your life in its completed form. Please let me clarify, vision is not based on where you are today, *"but"* rather on where you want to be in the near future. Vision is the completed version of a dream that starts or has started inside your mind. Your personal vision should be the end result of your total life plan. First you must have it clear in your mind what you want your life to be—complete with every detail. Then hit rewind to begin walking it out daily. This is very critical because every decision you make is made with the end result of your vision in mind. I have seen so many people that live their life on a "we'll see what happens" basis. "I'll just go to school and see what happens" or "I'll get married and just see what happens" or my favorite "I'll just get a job and see what happens." There are elements of risk or uncertainty in a vision *"but"* you must have an idea of what you want your life to end up like so you have some direction and clarity to make appropriate decisions that should guide you straight toward your destiny. If you don't stand for something you'll fall for anything. You may need to create a vision, improve or adjust *"but"* we all need to have a vision. It is a road map that drives anyone that is serious about success.

As little children, when we dreamed no one got jealous or envious. Everyone had a dream and all of our dreams had the potential to happen. No matter how big or how small they were, we respected everyone's dreams. How many jealous people do you know? A person can only get jealous when they are convinced that they can't achieve the same success, achieve the same goals or have a good life too. The innocence of a child and the unlimited potential protects them from ever getting jealous of someone else's vision. However, as adults we are trained to be mature and "realistic" and are often discouraged from going for our dreams and then become bitter when a friend or family member becomes successful at a high level. No wonder so many of us get bogged down into a boring everyday treadmill life, moving fast and going nowhere, feeling less than fulfilled. A treadmill life can only occur in the life of a person that has no vision. The lack of vision can lead to frustration, anger, anxiety, obesity, and depression. Do you know your ultimate vision for your life can still happen for you? "*But*' I'm too old." "*But*' it's too late." *ALL BUTS STINK!* It is never too late for you to successfully reach and live your vision. When you hear a person talk about their life, you can hear whether they have and are living their vision or if they have negotiated themselves out of their future. Have you negotiated yourself out of your vision? Have you negotiated yourself out of your future? Have you negotiated yourself out of your best life by being "realistic?"

Beware of a good idea.

Getting a clear vision for your life is hard to do, however sticking to your vision can be tougher. People often get sidetracked from their vision by getting derailed by a good idea. There is a difference between a good idea and a vision. We are not talking about good ideas in this book, we are talking about your vision. What has God put you on this earth to do? I believe that it is rather easy to confuse a good idea and a vision, so don't let pride get in your way of admitting the mistake if this sounds like you. I've had many of good ideas and acted on a few (that cost me a lot of time & money), *"but"* really had only one vision for my life. We all get good ideas from time to time. However, what is the ultimate vision you have for your life? What did God put you on this earth to do? Whatever that is, it is your vision. Good ideas will come and go, *"but"* a true vision keeps coming back to you. It stalks you day and night and there is no escape. I can honestly say that I am living the vision that I had as a child, almost to perfection. Yes! I was challenged many times to quit and I got distracted by a lot of good ideas, *"but"* my life took off once I connected to a vision for my life. I am honestly doing what God has placed me on this earth to do. You need to discover why you were put on this earth. Well, how do I discover why God created me? I will make a billion dollars once I make the fool proof formula to discover this age old mystery. However, I do know this. Your vision is correlated to your gift. Whatever you are destined to do you love to do it and you are very good at it. You are a natural at it. When a person is gifted in an area it is very easy for them to perform the task. It is easy for some people to sit at a piano and make it come to life. If I sit down at a piano I am liable to put the piano into an early death. Some people are natural leaders, inventors or creators. Some people were born to play golf or develop software. You have a gift, there is something that you do that comes easy to you and you are very good at it. Your vision will include the development and use of this gift. A gift is not something you decide, it is something you discover. Your gift is the foundational piece of your true vision.

If you don't know what your vision is you'll keep yourself busy until you find out or you'll just be busy the rest of your life. I hate seeing busy people who aren't living their vision. Being busy is the worst thing you can do. Busy with "stuff" can distract a person from living their best life. People who are just busy never seem happy or vibrant to me. I would be disinterested or unenergetic, too, if I wasn't living my vision. Busy people are always yapping on the cell phone, sending out e-mails, and are late for meetings because they are just so busy; yet no true progress is being made in their lives. We all have a few friends like this or know someone who fits this description. All you have to do is to look at a person's life in five-year increments and you can see if they truly have a personal vision. There were times early on in my life when I experienced a sense of being lost and living without a vision. This is a sign of immaturity; however, it doesn't have to be a lifestyle. Again, it took courage to recognize where I was and make some quick adjustments. If this applies to you, have the courage to admit it and search your heart until you have a true vision for your life. The best thing a parent can do for their child is to help them identify their natural gifting.

If you train yourself to listen to people talk about their lives, a simple conversation will reveal whether or not a person is living their vision. Most people will share intimate information concerning their lives and will reveal clues as to whether or not they are living their vision. If you hear a person and the undertone of their conversation is discouragement or regret, this is normally a red flag that they aren't living a vision or they are headed toward it *"but"* aren't quite there yet. A person with a vision has a certain drive to them, a focus, and can't be easily distracted. When a person has a real vision they don't stop until they get what they want. They are very focused and borderline obsessed. I wanted to play in the NBA so I would start my workouts at 5 a.m. and work out basically all day long. Other athletes would work out, *"but"* my workouts were designed with a vision in mind. While some athletes trained as if it would be nice if they made it to the NBA, I trained as if I was an NBA player already.

Vision keeps you focused. Vision keeps you excited. Vision allows you to be creative and innovative concerning the circumstances of your life. Vision improves your chances of making good decisions concerning your life. Every decision you make can be based on whether or not it affects your vision. Vision gives you power and focus like never before. How much has your life changed in the last five years? Are you living a focused life or just keeping busy?

Super size it!

Do you remember when you could go to fast food restaurants and super size your meal? Many fast food restaurants are getting away from their value meals. Did you super size when you had the chance? You're paying for the meal already, so why not add 49 cents and super size it? All you have to do is pay a little bit more. Do you know the same is true for your life? You can super size your vision and have a bigger life. You're already paying a price right now for the life you have. If your life isn't quite were you want it to be, there is one simple solution, pay a little bit more and you can have a bigger life. The price you need to pay to increase your vision may be a career change, going back to school, an investment of time, an investment of money, increased effort or focus or an investment in courage. You may need to create a vision all together because you never had one. In the pursuit of your vision, don't ever settle for less, don't quit until you get exactly what you want out of life without compromising your integrity or selling your family up a river.

I have found that settling for less is a national epidemic. Have you settled for less? Are you living the life you dreamed about? This is what happens to most people who settle for less. They are always busy *"but"* aren't going any where. They are working hard *"but"* never seem to get where they really want to be. Do you feel this way? You work much *"but"* reap very little and never really get fully satisfied. Something is missing. Have you noticed that your appetite will adjust to whatever you feed it? You must clearly identify exactly what you want professionally and personally so you can't be fooled by the results.

The key to super sizing your vision is courage. You must have courage to dream more. Your vision is yours, you must own it, your vision should drive your life. Vision is your very own intellectual property and must be protected at all cost as much as you protect your family, home and possessions. If your vision has been lost, stolen, or misplaced, you will lose your life and identity. YOU MUST GET IT BACK! We are being alerted of ways to avoid identity theft all the time. I know people that shred every document that comes into their home. I am afraid they will shred me if I stay there too long. I believe if you are not living your vision, your identity is a mystery, it has been stolen and compromised already. It is ok to shred those documents *"but"* please don't shred your vision by lacking courage.

This chapter is especially for the segment of our society that I call "average." They are average because they need to super size their vision *"but"* won't. Is this you? You like where you are *"but"* you know there is more out there for you. Do you know if you fit into this group that you can escape? Let's do it right now. Think about your life and how it would look super-sized. Can you see yourself with a happier family, more money, more fulfilling relationships, an advanced career, a larger home or a second home, or traveling the world? Take a good look at it! Doesn't it look good? You can have it. No one can stop you *"but"* you. All you have to do is pay a little more and you can get it.

I have learned that visions are defined by statements. For example, let's examine these two statements: "I hope to become a doctor." That's not a statement with any conviction. "I will become a doctor." Now that's a statement that is loaded with conviction. When you don't make statements you are not committed to your vision and you're just looking for one good excuse to quit. Visionaries make statements. They don't spend a lot of time pondering the "what ifs" they spend their energy, resources, and money figuring out how they will get it done.

You must have an appetite for success the same way in which a person who is hungry will not stop until they have eaten. Your vision has to be just as important as eating. That is the determination all successful people have who live their vision. Children have it early on. They will hound their parents until they get their way. I think it is a quality that is innate and critical to our success *"but"* our society teaches against it. Our society hasn't learned how to harness that drive without killing a child's spirit. I love my children's tenacity. It wears me out from time to time, *"but"* I hope they never lose it. It will serve them well later in life.

Barrier to Entry

A barrier that every high achiever must hurdle is Faith!!!! Can I really achieve this vision I dream about? Can my life really change and become all it can be? I know the answer to this question *"but"* it is important that you know it too. Do I have the faith it takes to endure the process of excellence or can I be discouraged out of it? Can I really achieve this vision? What happens if it doesn't work out? This is the number one reason most visions die. What happens if it doesn't work out? My thought is this: What happens if it does work out? You owe it to yourself to try. Don't live your life with regrets. A visionary can't be afraid to fail. If you pursue your true vision, it won't fail. You were put here on this earth to execute your vision. How could it fail? I want you to go way back to elementary school, high school or maybe even college, to the first day you took the job, opened for business, or said "I do," when you were still excited and your vision was crystal clear. What was that vision? The key is the statement you make after this very important question. Whatever statement you make right now will make or break everything. It's powerful!!! Your vision isn't real until you make the statement after the question. What is your personal vision? You must make a statement right now. I will become a lawyer...I will become a doctor...I will become an entrepreneur... my marriage will last...I will travel the world. Make a statement concerning your vision and watch out. Whatever statement you make you will become.

Go somewhere quiet and write your vision down so you can actually see it on paper. It should be in the same file or area of your goals. Actually, they should be one and the same. Your goals are merely pit stops or checkpoints along the way to your vision. You owe it to yourself to create a real vision on something you can see, so grab a tablet or write it in your laptop. When you write it down, it is transferred from your mind to reality and the moment the ink dries it becomes real. Don't let what you wrote on your paper out of your sight. Take it out every week, every month and every year. Look at it, meditate on it, study it, tweak it, and handle it like a road map for success. When you wake up in the morning make sure your vision is top on your list as you start your day. You are the only person who can carry out your vision. Society needs you to execute your vision. *"But'* do I really need to do this?" Yes! *ALL BUTS STINK!* Society needs your vision to become reality.

Time is not something
you spend. Time is a
very valuable commodity
that should be invested.

— *Walter Bond*

CHAPTER FIVE

Don't Waste Your Time! Invest It!

Time is not something you spend. Time is a very valuable commodity that should be invested. Don't ever spend your time again--invest it. If you develop this mindset your life will take a very different course. I have seen too many busy people in my short lifetime. I would love to see more productive people living their dream life. I guarantee that you are mindful of your cell phone minutes and your frequent flyer miles. What should be your biggest concern: cell phone minutes, frequent flyer miles, or life minutes? You can waste time a couple of hours a week going to lunch with the wrong people, focusing on the wrong things at work, watching hours of unproductive television, and doing any number of non-productive activities. Stop wasting your time. It's the most valuable asset you possess.

Here's a popular statement-- *"Life is not fair."* Do you agree or disagree with this statement? I know one element of life that is totally fair and that is TIME. Time is as fair as it can get. Time is not prejudiced; it doesn't discriminate or play politics. Think about it! We all get 24 hours a day no matter where we live, our ethnic background, heritage, religion, or our demographics. We all have 24 hours a day to live. Time does not delay or hesitate; it knows no race, no man, or people. Time doesn't even know or care to know your name. It has a job to do and that is to keep on moving without hesitation or disruption. Time could be an awesome motivational speaker. Couldn't you hear her? "No one can stop me, I am unstoppable." How well do you invest **your** time?

The most critical element in time management is giving yourself time limits in which to complete tasks. If a job should take fifteen minutes, then allow fifteen minutes of your day to get it done. The mistake many people make is that they take way too much time to complete simple activities. When we are efficient with our time, we will learn that 24 hours a day is plenty of time in which to create a life of wealth, happiness, balance and abundance.

I can remember early in my professional business career, I had scheduled a lunch with an extremely successful businessman named Phil. At that time, he was an executive with a telecommunications company located in the upper Midwest. As we sat down to meet, he took his watch off of his wrist and set it down on the table. He informed me before we started the meeting that he only had an hour to spend for lunch and he pulled out a timer setting it for an hour. We were having a great conversation *"but"* the table was full of clocks, stopwatches, and all kinds of gadgets and I could hear this subtle ticking sound the entire meeting. We talked about business, family, religion, and politics when all of a sudden his timer went off. The conversation was going great. I could have stayed there all day if it had been up to me and I assumed he would ignore his timer and continue the conversation. However, when his timer went off, he closed the meeting abruptly and was off within two minutes. It felt weird. I felt cheated. I almost called 911 because I felt violated and abandoned. Surely there must be something criminal in this since no one had ever done that to me before. Besides, I assumed the conversation was so good that he would shut his timer off and we would finish what we started. If it were up to me, that is exactly what I would have done. That's what most of the people I know would have done. In my mind we weren't finished, *"but"* in his mind we were. He allotted one hour to invest in lunch and when that hour was up he had the courage and discipline to end it. He had other things to do and if he allowed our time to spill over, it would have affected the rest of his productive day.

I have observed Phil's career and met again with him on a few occasions and he always mentions what a great time he has when we go to lunch; so I know he likes me and enjoys getting together, *"but"* he still pulls out his stopwatch, *"but"* now I know the drill. I make sure I make the most out of the hour he invests in me. He is such a successful person and someone I look up to as a mentor. He is now the president of two companies, in two different states. He commutes between the west coast and the Midwest for both companies each month. When the last company hired him, a part of the deal was a gorgeous property in California with a beautiful mountain right in the middle of an acreage lot where he could build his dream home. The CEO of the company gave him the mountain right next to his. I know people have offered you great jobs, *"but"* has anyone ever offered you a mountain? How does he do it? He manages and invests his time wisely. He doesn't spend his time--he invests it, and he allots the proper amount of time to each activity and won't deviate from it. Phil has a happy marriage and two beautiful daughters who are college graduates.

They are normal, happy children with no apparent issues that you can sometimes run into with high-level executives' children. Phil's has it all simply because he knows how to invest his time.

You must understand and accept that 24 hours is a long time if you are efficient with your time. If you sleep eight hours a day, that leaves sixteen hours for you to do whatever else you deem important. How many times have you heard a person say, "There is just not enough time in the day?" Not true! There is plenty of time in the day to do just about anything. "I would have done it, *'but'* I ran out of time." ***ALL BUTS STINK!*** You just didn't manage your time wisely.

Before you can understand how you spend your time, you need to understand your own personal vision and value system. On the chart provided below, I want you to fill out the time schedule so you can see how your average day is spent. You need to see what your average day looks like from the time you wake up to the time you go to bed.

5 AM_____

6 AM_____

7 AM_____

8 AM_____

9 AM_____

10 AM_____

11 AM _____

12 PM_____

1 PM _____

2 PM _____

3 PM _____

4 PM _____

5 PM _____

6 PM _____

7 PM _____

8 PM _____

9 PM _____

10 PM _____

11 PM _____

12 AM _____

1 AM _____

2 AM _____

3 AM _____

4 AM _____

I want you to write down the time you get up in the morning and every activity you do during the entire day. Be very detailed so you can see where all your time is going. This should be an average weekday. Don't concern yourself with the weekend right now. If you do a good job with your five work days, you can spend the weekend doing whatever. By completing this time line, you should be able to gain some valuable insight regarding your day and it should help give you some clarity on how you can make your day more productive. The average person makes excuses about not working out because they are too busy. I guarantee that as you look at your daily schedule, you will be able to find some time to work out. How about giving up that favorite TV show you watch every night? What is going to give you a better return on your investment, an hour of physical fitness that could improve your overall health and quality of life or CSI? If you need to spend more time with your spouse, don't tell me that as you look at your schedule you can't find the time? There is tremendous value for you to look back on your day and discover how you invested your time. If you need to make some adjustments, do it now.

If there is some discrepancy in making adjustments with your daily schedule, I have a simple exercise you can do to locate your value system. On the following page I would like you to write down your personal value system. Rank in order the top five areas of your life that are most important to you: God, family, work, and so on.

My personal value system

1.

2.

3.

4.

5.

Once you are done, I want you to cross reference both lists to see if your daily schedule is congruent with your value system. My job is not to tell you how to invest your time because only you can do that. Everyone has a different value system. Make sure you are aware of where you are investing your time and make sure it is consistent with your value system. The amazing phenomenon is that many people have daily schedules that aren't congruent with their own personal value system and refuse to change.

I tend to believe what you **do** more than what you **say**. In other words, your value system can be found in your daily schedule. We all have been conditioned with politically correct answers concerning our own personal value system. Most of us will say God, family, then work. This sounds very good and politically correct *"but"* is an outright lie in many cases. However, what does your time sheet communicate? Which list do you believe communicates your value system most accurately? If you can be honest with yourself and have the courage to find errors and make the necessary adjustments, you will be able to make huge strides toward living a life that is productive--one that is consistent with your value system and vision.

When the bulk of your time has been invested according to your own value system, there should be good balance in your life and you should have an internal peace that nothing important in your life is being neglected. Everyone is busy and the day can end before we are able to get everything done. That is why we need to clearly define our value system so we don't run out of time to do the most important things. I want to encourage you to take inventory of your time every few months. It's so easy to get caught up in the hustle of life and let things get out of whack.

How much time do you waste on areas of your life that aren't in your top five? How much time do you waste on a daily basis on things that will not give you a good return on your investment? You may waste time watching unproductive television, or having unproductive conversations on the phone with unproductive people. Always be aware of time thieves--they are everywhere.

A time thief could be spending too much time on a hobby, with a friend or family member, or it could be your job. Of course, if you overextend yourself, you will have time issues. If your schedule is planned out well, when an opportunity comes along, you can clearly see that you just don't have the time to waste and you can always blame your productive schedule. It will be much easier to say no when you have a schedule you respect and follow. If you don't respect your time, don't expect others to either.

How much you value and maximize your time will dictate your quality of life. Imagine a time bank? Once you make a deposit in the time bank with unused time, you can clearly see the balance of time in your monthly statements *"but"* it is gone forever. You couldn't use this time again, it would just sit there for you to review. Your statement would come in the mail the same day your bank statement comes, so you could see it as a reminder of how much time you wasted that month. I would love to see my account. I would hope it would be empty, *"but"* I too believe and know that I have wasted some of my own precious time and I can't get it back. This is one account we would want to be on zero. In terms of time not wasted, we would all love to file bankruptcy. We all have wasted time in some way or another. I believe this new and unique account would motivate everyone to be mindful of time, and we would change our habits if we could visually see how we have spent our time--how much we have invested correctly, and how many poor investments we have made with our time.

If we look at time the same way we look at money, we could take advice from a financial planner, they always preach the value of investing money in something that will bring a good return on your investment. We would hear words like stocks, bonds, mutual funds, and real estate. They would never advise us to invest money on anything that would not give a decent return on our money. They would never encourage us to invest in anything that doesn't give a return at all. They would ask, "Why put your money at risk?" A wealthy person consistently puts money into investments that bring a good return and over time they are rich. In time, they reap the financial benefits of their investments. Shouldn't we look at time the same way we look at money? What would happen to your life if every moment of your time you invested into the opportunities, careers, and people that would give you a good return on your investment? You don't have the slightest idea how much your life could change if you only invested in activities, tasks and people that give you a good return on your investment.

I can remember another monumental experience that taught me the importance of time from a very successful person. When I began to investigate the speaking industry as a career, I made contact with a very famous speaker named Desi Williamson. He is a Hall of Fame speaker based in Minneapolis. It was an awesome experience for me because when he returned my initial call, he informed me that we were related--we were actually cousins. What? I thought this was too weird. After a brief conversation on the phone, I asked if we could meet for lunch being I wanted to become a professional speaker too. I knew there was no one more qualified than he. His first question was, "Are you serious about the speaking business? I can't afford for you to waste my time." I was offended at first. I had never heard anyone be so blunt. I replied, "Yes, I am very serious." So we scheduled lunch and he mapped out the speaking business for me on a sheet of paper and promised me that if I followed the plan he could help collapse time frames for me in the development of my speaking business. This encounter with Desi was so critical to my business development and it taught me a lesson of how truly successful people operate. Desi was not being rude. He was merely protecting his most valuable asset—TIME. I am sure others have wasted his time in the past. Later on as my business grew, Desi let me know he was proud of me and was impressed that I actually executed what he so clearly mapped out for me. He told me that after 15 years in the speaking business I was the only speaker he invested time in who actually acted on the information he gave. At the time I found that to be very strange *"but"* now I know how true it is. I am now approached by more people than you can believe who want me to help them become a professional speaker. However, I don't mind investing time in a person that wants to be a professional speaker *"but"* I need to make quick judgments on whether or not this person is a good investment of my time. I don't mind investing my time in people, it's what I do. However, I am aware of time thieves and so I protect my time diligently, because it is my most valuable asset.

I believe you are pretty logical and should understand my points pretty well. If you want to improve your value in your industry, guess what? You need to invest more time in it. Get to work early sometimes, stay late sometimes. Read more books, reports, and journals, concerning your industry. Invest some time in attending seminars, join an association, and become an industry leader and network with the best in your industry. You can't become the best if you don't invest the time and energy it takes to become the best. Many of you never even heard of me as a professional basketball player, I am not offended because I have never heard of you either. However, I can't even calculate how many hours I invested to become a professional in the NBA that you never heard of.

If you want to improve your marriage or family, guess what? Invest more time in your spouse. Take your spouse on a romantic weekend, go to a marriage seminar, stop investing time with your girlfriend or mistress or the milk man and spend all your time with your spouse. Invest some time going on dates, go to a movie, or go horseback riding. You can rediscover why you got married in the first place. Invest the time you need to get the return on all your critical relationships. If your life is hectic it could be because you are not disciplined with your time. Maybe you try to do too many things while neglecting the most important things. You need to be organized and live according to a value system and schedule so nothing is out of whack or neglected. Don't tell me how much you love your family and you never spend time with them. I know people that are committed to investing 30 minutes a day running to Starbucks and won't sit down and invest 30 minutes a day talking with their own children. Let me ask you a question, what will give you a better return on your investment Starbucks or your kids?

Nothing can heal your home faster than spending quality time with each member of your family. Invest an appropriate amount of time with your family and loved ones. Take family vacations, sign your kids up for football, basketball, and soccer, and go to their games cheering like crazy--win or lose. Have a movie night, game night, go camping, play tennis. Sign them up for ballet and make a big deal about the recital and be there cheering like a fanatic. You can't have a good relationship with anyone without investing a lot of time building the relationship. If your husband complains that there is not enough hanky panky, schedule it!!!!! Turn it into a periodic appointment that meets his/her need or expectation of frequency. If you know your wife likes to go for walks, schedule it. If your mechanic needs to see you every six months for service, your spouse needs some service too. You need to do some yard work? Schedule it like an appointment. Many of you have a hard time saying no to people--you little people pleaser-- time thieves steal your precious time away and you can't get it back. I now have the answer for you. If you have everything scheduled, you can always blame your schedule. No one will argue with a schedule or even question what the appointment is.

If you want to get in better physical shape because you are not happy with your body, guess what? You need to invest time in the gym working out or doing research on how to eat healthy and spend less time and money investing in junk food. If you invest your time in good things, things that line up with your personal value system and vision, I guarantee you will get great returns on your investment of time. *"But'* there is not enough time in the day." *ALL BUTS STINK!* There is plenty of time in a day, if you invest your time wisely.

Teach them young

It is so important for us to teach our children about not wasting time. Are your children investing time in things that don't give them a good a return on their investment? I was speaking at a high school a few years ago and I asked the students by a show of hands how many play video games more than two hours a day. The response was about 65%-75%. Four hours a day? The response was about 35%. I asked who plays video games at least 6 hours a day? One young man named David raised his hand. I called him down front and asked him how many hours a day he played video games? He told me that he played every day after school from 3-9p.m. Then I asked him his GPA... No comment, of course. I didn't mean to embarrass him or the room, for that matter, *"but"* I needed to take this opportunity to teach a lesson because video games have become an epidemic with our youth. Video games are raising our children. David was a very bright young man and I knew he would get it. "David, what would happen to your grades if you spent three hours playing video games and three hours doing homework? Wouldn't you be a straight A student?" He smiled and said, "Of course." I then asked him what kind of return on his investment in time would video games give him? He replied, "None." I think I connected with David that day, and the whole class, for that matter. I would love to see David's parents' time sheet. The real reason he played video games so much was that his mom and dad were not investing time with him. I think video games are entertaining *"but"* shouldn't be used by parents as a babysitting tool just because they are too lazy or too busy to invest in their own child's development. I bet they would answer politically correct if I asked them the five most important things in their lives.

The fact of the matter is that everyone from Bill Gates, Oprah, and George Bush to that homeless person you saw on your way to work today holding that universal homeless sign "Will work for food," gets the same 24 hours in a day. I often wonder what would happen if a homeless person invested their time better. In fact, the next time I drop off a buck or some change into their hands I will offer some advice on how they may improve their situation by investing their time better. How and where you invest your time is so critical to your success. If you really think about it, 24 hours is a long time if we invest our time in the right things. Invest your time appropriately in the five most important components of your life. Only spend the appropriate amount of time allotted toward an activity and, please, whatever you do, don't ever waste your time, if you can help it. Time is not something you spend, it is something you invest. When you respect your time, others will too. There should be no more excuses with how you spend your time. *"'But'* I ran out of time"....*ALL BUTS STINK!* I don't want to hear it, invest your time wisely.

CHAPTER SIX

Set Goals That Create Pressure

Goals create more than a road map for your success. Goals create the element of pressure you need to become successful. Goals can rescue you from the dreaded *comfort zone*. I think the *comfort zone* is a dangerous epidemic sweeping America at a record pace. I think many people that live in this great country never reach their potential because of the *comfort zone*. Many people shy away from goals because they don't like the pressure goals create. Success doesn't come by accident. I don't believe that successful people are lucky. The are very talented at what they do *"but"* for the most part--they are great goal setters. The pressure created by effective goal setting is exactly what you need to get your life moving in the right direction. No goals--no pressure. No pressure--no great thing can be accomplished. Great people are great because they expect more out of themselves than others expect out of them. Great people are great because they set their goals high enough to propel them to higher levels of excellence than the norm. If you become an effective goal setter, you must do things differently. Setting new goals every year will force you to grow and to operate at a higher level. If your life hasn't changed in the last five years, it is because you haven't set many goals or you really didn't shoot for the goals you did set. You've been so busy the last five years, haven't you? Everyone in our society is busy. However, being busy does not equate to being productive. Setting goals protects us from the unproductive trap of being busy. I can't imagine my life without goals. Many people that are what I call "average" are only "average" because they haven't made goal setting a part of their life. I couldn't stomach my life being exactly the same every year, I expect myself to be better every single year I am alive. I expect to be a better person, husband, father, speaker, author and business person every single year. How do I achieve this? I am glad you asked.....I set goals every year and let them drive my life.

Here are three keys to goal setting.

I. Write it on tablets.

You must write your goals down. When you talk about them they are just hopes and dreams, *"but"* when you write your goals down they become real. Once these goals are set in stone in your heart and on paper, write them in a journal, PC, laptop, or anywhere you can easily refer to them. Put them on the wall in your office, on your refrigerator, or put them on a screen-saver—anywhere that is visible. Go to Kinko's and make a big poster of your goals and put it up on the wall of your home or office. You must be able to see your goals on a daily basis. It is critical that you don't hide them. Out of sight is out of mind! You must see your goals so you can stay focused on them every day. Don't focus on Oprah, CSI, or American Idol because they can't take you anywhere like staying focused on your goals can. If you keep your goals in your sight on a daily basis, you won't keep doing the same things the same way.

Setting goals is the only way you will change your daily activities. If you change your daily activities you can move closer toward your goals. If your goals aren't in plain view, it is too easy to keep doing everything the same way you've been doing them the last few years. The key to goal setting is a simple exercise in writing them down and keeping them in your sight.

Every week check your goals and make sure you are on target. Many people check once a month or even once a quarter. I don't believe in that. If you check only once a month it will be three months before you realize you may be behind and the year is a quarter over. When you have weekly goals you can't get too far off track without making some changes. When you check every week you stay aggressive and this keeps you in the driver's seat. This gives you time to switch gears and use your creativity and innovation to get yourself back on track, if needed. If your vision is real to you, why wouldn't you look at it every day and refer to it all the time. This may sound obsessive to you, well maybe it is *"but"* I don't know any successful people that aren't borderline obsessive with their vision. I don't want you to get off balance and you won't if you have a balanced vision that covers your total life. The bottom line is this, you must write it down so it will stay fresh in your mind and set in your subconscious.

II. Tell everyone you know.

Tell everyone you trust about your goals. Make your goals public knowledge. This will accomplish two things: first this makes you accountable, and you need accountability in order to achieve your goals. It doesn't do you any good to keep your goals to yourself because it's too easy to quit. Why? If you quit, no one will ever know you didn't achieve your goals. Have you ever worked out with a workout buddy? It's easy to quit a workout plan when you work out by yourself because no one knows that you blew off your workout, *"but"* when you have to call your workout buddy and explain that you are about to blow-off a workout, it is tougher because now your flakiness is public knowledge. Typically, we hate to let people down, including ourselves. There is a powerful force created when you share a goal with someone else. You don't have to share these goals with everyone, I recommend only the right people…only those you trust. Please don't share your goals with anyone in your life who may discourage you or make light of them. We all need support, so tell your catalysts and advocates what your goals are. Goals get others excited, your support system will then cheer you on, motivate you, or give you information that can assist you in your efforts. This will also help you identify your true friends and create a support network for you, which is the second accomplishment for making your goals public. Have you ever been to a marathon? Everyone there has a support system to keep them going. It is rare that you see someone at a marathon alone. I have spoken to a few runners and they will tell you how many times they thought about quitting from the 20th to the 26th mile. Often these support networks help the runners in their training, during the race, and right up to the finish line. Every time you visit with an advocate, they will ask you how's it going? You may run into them at a coffee shop, a school assembly, or at a gas station and they will ask you for an update each time they see you. This will keep your motor running. If you see them while you are focused, this will create the energy you need to keep going. If you have lost some focus and are off task of your goals, when you see them, allow the emotional guilt of feeling like a flake to motivate you to get back on track.

III. Take a year-end break.

Once you have completed an entire year, don't just dive right into the next year without an evaluation of the year. In fact, I am in the process of writing a book called "*The off-season.*" You probably have done an awesome job achieving some of your goals, some of your goals you may have slightly missed, and a few of your goals you may not even be close to reaching. The reality is this: professional athletes have an **off-season**, why not you? Take a few days off, or a long weekend, and evaluate your year by looking at each goal you set for the year. This is what I call an **off-season**. During this time, evaluate your year and give yourself an overall grade for every goal you set out to accomplish. Ask yourself some critical questions. Why did I reach the goals I set? Why didn't I reach some of the goals I set? How could I have reached these goals sooner? Did I set this goal too high? Did I set this goal too low? Then set your new goals for the upcoming year and build on what you have accomplished. Use your creativity and innovation and take some time to evaluate what you can do better to reach your goals for the next year.

The **off-season** concept can be the key to your future. If you use this technique effectively, every year you will be a peak performer and the most-improved person you know. Live your life in one-year segments and make sure you don't let your years run together. If I didn't learn anything else as a professional athlete, I learned that each and every season is a new season. What happened last year, good or bad, has nothing to do with the next season. How can a person ever get bored, become stagnant, or depressed if they do a good job of setting goals each year. "*But*' I can't afford to take the time to take an **off-season**." *ALL BUTS STINK!* You can't afford not to. I have heard that Bill Gates takes any where from

7-10 days and goes away to some remote place and thinks about how Microsoft can impact the industry of technology. That is what I call an *off-season*, I know what you are thinking—he is Bill Gates he can afford to take an *off-season*. My point is that don't you think these *off-season* breaks are the reason he is Bill Gates in the first place. Many people argue that they can't afford to take an *off-season*, my argument is that you can't afford not to. If you don't take an *off-season* to evaluate your year, you run the risk of being the same person you were last year. Your life is a reflection of you, if that is true I can't afford to be the same person next year, if I expect to achieve greater success.

If you make every decision based on how you want your life to look five years from now, your life will be much different five years from now. You must take some time away from the rat race. Going to Disneyland and spending time with the biggest rat of them all—Mickey Mouse—doesn't count. An *off-season* is not a vacation; an *off-season* is when you work at your work. I promise you that your *off-season* will be the key to nailing all your goals each year and you will reach your vision. You may struggle with this the first year, *"but"* make it a lifestyle, and before you know it your life will be even more awesome than it is already. My next book will be called *"The off-season,"* that is how much I believe in the concept. My goal with this book is to challenge our culture as we know it, instead of just giving an employee two weeks vacation I believe that all employees should get an *off-season* break as a part of their benefits package.

Pressure brings out the best and the worst in all of us, which is a good thing--at least you're out and there should me no confusion of who you are under pressure. You need to know the real you so you can improve yourself. Pressure will always reveal your true character. Successful people don't mind pressure, some even love it. If you don't like pressure, this is your chance to change your mind and embrace it. How do you respond to pressure? Do you hate to feel pressure? Do you ever put pressure on yourself? Do you always play it safe? You can take the easy way out and never set goals or you can enter the world of excellence by giving yourself to its proven power.

Warning!

I do believe that personal pressure caused by setting goals can be taken too far and can turn into self-abuse if we are setting goals based on fantasy and not on reality. This is rare *"but"* it can happen. Remember I work with thousands of people in an average week. The most common problem I have seen working with people is that they don't set goals and fail to execute this simple fundamental of success. A good goal can create a healthy expectation of yourself and personal awareness. Goal-setting is meant to be enjoyable. When it becomes laborious, you're not going about it the right way.

Some people set goals so high they will never reach them; then they live in condemnation their entire life. We have seen the other extreme where people set goals so low they get a false sense of accomplishment and are never really challenged. We are all blessed with raw talents and gifts, *"but"* without the right amount of pressure that is created by goals, none of us will ever reach our potential. That is why effective goal-setting is so important. It is the only way you can really become unstoppable. Goals also create an unbelievable amount of focus, which is the most powerful aspect of goal-setting. When a person has embraced their goals, every morning they wake up very focused.

Goals and visions must co-exist in our life. I believe vision is the end result, *"but"* goals are the pit stops along the way to your vision. A person should create a personal vision complete with details first. Then hit rewind in their life right back to where they are today, and then figure out what steps it will take to walk out the vision that was created in their mind. For example, I want to have a multi-million-dollar seminar company with several different business units. I can see it--the office, staff, conferences, and keynotes--helping thousands of companies, organizations, and families, every year. I must hit rewind from that vision in my head all the way back to where I am today and then begin to walk out the vision daily. You should always set goals that will move you toward your vision. This should make sense!!! Your life can look drastically different five years from now if you execute. Set goals for the year that line up with an overall vision for your life. You can set goals concerning your career, weight, personal or family life, and have faith--it can happen to you. Let these goals be your focus for the entire year and have confidence they will lead you to your vision.

When you set goals the only person you have to fight is you. This is where the true battle takes place. I believe that NO ONE CAN STOP YOU BUT YOU!!! You can blame other people and get yourself off the hook *"but"* never forget the truth. Goals spark creativity inside all of us. Goals force us to change and improve. It is an amazing phenomenon. Once we set a goal our brain starts to work. You see it happen all of the time no matter the experience. It can happen for your company, family, youth group, or church. In fact, when you see organizations digress into fighting and squabbling, it is because the organization has no clear goals or vision. If you don't set goals you'll never know what your life could have been.

Set your goals, write them down somewhere so you can see them, keep them in your mind, and meditate on them day and night. Let your mind work and before you know it your life will resemble exactly what you expected. Remember to share your goals with your spouse, your boss, coach, advocate, and catalysts. We all need a little encouragement from time to time, including those of us who are motivational speakers. Always create a community of support and accountability; no one can be successful alone. If you ever get down or a little discouraged you will be surprised how much strength you can gain from others who stand in support of your goals. Also, take a break each year and prepare to engage the next year with a whole new set of goals. Goals are the easiest and most effective way for you to create the life you want. *"But"* I tried to set goals and they don't work." *ALL BUTS STINK!* If they don't work, you didn't do it right. Goal-setting is a task that is fundamental to success.

Remember that Rome was not built in a day. I want to remind you of an old Asian proverb. The best time to plant a tree was twenty years ago. The second best time to plant a tree is today. It is never too late to make changes in your life. If you master the art of effective goal-setting you will be unstoppable.

What people say about you on a daily basis is how you are branded in your community.

– Walter Bond

CHAPTER SEVEN

Build Your Brand Like A Star

Our society has been saturated by all of the slogans, brands, and micro brands that big corporations use to sell their products and/or services. "We love to see you smile." Sound familiar to anyone? "Always lowest prices, always." Any guesses? "When it absolutely positively has to be there overnight." Give up yet? Ok...Ok McDonald's, Wal-Mart & Federal Express. You may like or dislike these companies *"but"* you can't argue that they have built great brands and that millions of people use their products and services. These corporations are household names. What comes to mind when you think about their name? Has your experience been what they had hoped for? What about the companies and products you have come to trust over the years? What toothpaste do you use? What brand of clothes do you buy? What hotels do you prefer? Companies have made billions and billions of dollars by developing their brand into household names. They will continue to make billions as long as they keep their brand strong. Isn't there a lesson in all this for us? Companies are always investing time and money to maintain, strengthen and improve their brand. Shouldn't we take our professional brand just as serious? What comes to your peers' mind when your name comes up?

The reality of the situation is this: whether you like it or not, you are a corporation. A mini corporation, true enough, *"but"* how well you develop your brand will dictate how big or small your mini corporation is. You must invest time and money to improve your brand. Have you even thought about your professional brand? Ever wondered why you always have job options or opportunities? You may have an excellent brand and never even thought about it. You were just being you. Unfortunately you may have a poor or mediocre brand because you were just being you and you are always looking for a new job or you are rarely considered for promotions when they become available. I want you to start thinking about your professional brand and how you are positioned in the marketplace, because your value in the marketplace is at stake. We all have a brand that we have developed over time; however strong or weak our brand is, it has already been established. The biggest boost your career can get is for you to totally focus on developing the quality of your professional brand.

A company's brand is the combination of what they say about themselves in their marketing and advertising, and what the consumer says based on their experiences using the product or service. When what a company says about themselves lines up with what the consumer experiences--Jackpot! That is when you have the makings of a very strong brand. When there is a discrepancy or conflict between the two, we will have a problem with the strength and quality of the brand. What is your professional brand at work? What value do you believe you bring to your company or industry daily? Would your employer and co-workers agree and say the same thing you say about yourself? Is there a discrepancy? When you say a company's name, we all have an opinion or thought about that company based on our personal experience with them. If not, we will rely on the opinions of our family and friends, and will hold their thoughts in high esteem. Sometimes we give them a thumbs-up, sometimes it's a thumbs-down and sometimes it's lukewarm. How many times have you avoided a restaurant, vendor or person based on what others have said about them? You respect them so much that you never give the product or person a chance based on what you have already heard about them. We won't even give a company or product any consideration if we hear something negative from a trusted person. We hear people's opinions all the time and it influences our perception of people and in business it influences where we invest our money

Because we all have big mouths, we will talk about products and services when given the opportunity. The only thing we talk about more than products or services is people. People love to talk about people. This is a powerful phenomenon that is a part of human nature. So, if that is the case, shouldn't you use this to your advantage? Everyone you know will talk about you when given the chance. Why not make sure you influence what they say about you? What people say about you on a daily basis is how you are branded in your community. With every personal encounter we have, we create our own personal sales force or wrecking crew of our personal and professional brand. The most powerful form of advertising is word of mouth. Any company would agree with this. It is the intangible that either makes or breaks the success of a company, organization, or in this case, a person. You may have your job right now because of your brand. You may have met your husband or wife because of your brand. Conversely, we never know what we may have missed out on because of something someone said about us that wasn't good or was less than favorable about us that was detrimental to our brand. I don't want to put you in bondage worrying about what people think and say about you, *"but"* I want you to understand that your brand is on the line every day. How strong is your professional brand today? Is what you believe about your brand consistent with what people experience when they interact with you?

There are six keys to developing and improving your personal brand.

I. Become an expert.

The first and most important key is to **become an expert** in your industry. This is the most important key in building your professional brand. Our society esteems experts and nothing can increase your value more. It's simple! Perfect your craft!!! Our society has become so lazy very few people are willing to pay the price to master their skill, and it doesn't happen overnight. To become an expert takes a long-term commitment. It can mean going back to school for an additional degree, attending more workshops or seminars, coming in an hour early or staying an hour late, *"but"* commit yourself to learning, perfecting, and knowing as much as you can about your industry. I say it all the time, when I left sports and entered corporate America I couldn't believe how lazy people were. There are very few people committed to becoming the best in the world at what they do. The funny part of the whole deal is this, I see mediocre people go to watch professional athletes and have the nerve to criticize. Until you become the best in the world at what you do, keep your mouth shut.

II. Dress/Look Good.

You can typically look at a person who is successful because there is a certain quiet confidence that illuminates from them. How many times have you just looked at a person and you just knew they were someone very successful. Now, of course, this isn't always the case, *"but"* how you look is very important. The moment someone sees you they make an assessment and place a value on you. After they get to know you better, their perception can change, *"but"* that first impression is their point of reference. A job interview doesn't begin when you answer the interview questions, it begins when you enter the room. Always look your best. This includes grooming yourself and good hygiene, as well as the clothes you choose. The best way to improve your wardrobe inexpensively is to shop out of season. Every season all of the department stores have to make room for new inventory, so you can find name-brand clothing and shoes at a great discount. You may have to wait a season to wear your new clothes *"but"* you will still be in style and looking good without going broke. Always look your best. When you look good you feel good and everyone will respond to you in a very different way.

III. Live with integrity.

Your integrity is like your grade point average (GPA)--every day you get a grade. If you tell someone you're going to do something, do it. This builds trust from your peers and your brand needs trust. Be reliable and trustworthy with information, thoughts, and possessions, always do the right thing. Every day we have choices and I believe our choices are represented by our lives. One bad choice can damage your integrity, which will surely damage your brand. We all make mistakes, *"but"* when you do own up to it, apologize quickly and move on. Protect your integrity like a GPA--one F can destroy it. We all have seen celebrities with unbelievable brands that are destroyed overnight by some scandal. Even if they were found innocent, their brand was weakened none-the-less. The moment your integrity is compromised your brand is compromised. The good news is that you can repair your brand when it is compromised over time *"but"* do whatever you can to avoid damaging your brand. Please avoid using foul language. Cursing can be offensive and the person offended may never say a word to you *"but"* make a mental note. This can hurt your brand as well as excessive drinking at company events. I can't tell you how many events I have been to that I have heard people introduce people and mention how much they drink at company events and do outlandish things in the name of fun. These people are always likeable and the life of the party. However, they rarely command the respect they need to get promoted or viewed as a person worthy of leadership. Have a good time, enjoy yourself, be the life of the party, not its conversation the next morning.

IV. Keep a clean home/ office/car.

Your office, home, and car are a reflection of your personality. You want to have a great representation in these three different areas. The people who impress me the most are those who have clean homes, offices, and cars, even when you know you surprised them and popped in unexpected. We all clean up pretty good when we know company is coming *"but"* that isn't real or authentic. Cleanliness in those areas of your life is a subtle way to strengthen your brand without people ever articulating a word. When you see a person who is filthy, it makes a statement about their organizational skills, performance, and character. Keep these areas of your life clean as much as possible. I had a neighbor that I lived next to for eleven years and their home looked just as new as the day they bought it. If they ever put their home up for sale, all they would need to do is stick a sign in the yard. Their home is immaculate all the time. I have always respected them for how clean they have kept their home, yard and cars for years.

V. Develop good communication skills.

Communication is a great way to reveal to your peers who you are. People often associate your communication skills with intelligence. Again, this isn't always the case, *"but"* when a person communicates well and uses proper grammar, it is a great representation of an intelligent and well-informed person. This is a great way to increase your value over time. An effective communicator is always valued in a corporate environment. A person can be a complete fraud without a brain. However, if they are good communicators it will take a long time for anyone to figure out how dumb they may be. Speak well, be polite, and always look directly into a person's eyes. Do you always look people in the eyes when you talk to them? Many people struggle having good eye contact. It has been said that your eyes are the gateway to your soul. Always look a person in the eye. It builds their confidence in you and can help you gain a better understanding of the person with whom you are communicating. It will also help you become a good listener. The listener is in control of the conversation. I wish there were courses in school we could take on being a good listener. Listening is critical because it allows you to accumulate information. The more information you possess, the more valuable you are, and if you are the listener you leave the conversation with the most information and power in the relationship. Most people are poor listeners having never been taught how to listen, the importance of listening or could simply care less about you or what you have to say. Most people's communication patterns is to wait for the other person to shut up so they can hear themselves talk. You can improve your brand by becoming an effective communicator and 50% of communication is simply listening. Most wives biggest complaint about their husband is that they don't listen and it drives wives crazy.

VI. Confidence is arrogance under control.

We all should push the pendulum of confidence as far as we can without crossing the line into arrogance. You will never operate at your full potential without confidence. However, don't ever become arrogant because arrogant people stop growing and developing because they think they have arrived. Confidence is based on how you think and what you believe about yourself. Some people don't think well of themselves and this destroys confidence. Think well of yourself and develop good work ethics. I have never seen a hard worker struggle with confidence. If you struggle with confidence, it's because you are lazy. The sure fire way of improving your confidence is by hard work. Begin working hard to overcome your lack of confidence and your confidence is sure to grow. If you don't have confidence in how you look, work harder at it. All you have to do is to wake up earlier and work harder when you get dressed. In today's marketplace you can invest in your looks and make yourself look better. You can buy fake hair, nails and body parts to get the job done. The bottom line is this, if you lack confidence in anything—work harder at it.

How much value have you created for yourself at this point in your life? Well, I have a hint for you. What salaries were you offered when you were in the market for a job? I guarantee your offers have all been in the same range. Very few people get offers all over the board. Some people are offered $8 an hour, $80,000 a year, some get over $800,000 a year offers on a consistent basis. We must understand—whether we like it or not—that we all have a brand and we either weaken or strengthen our personal brand on a daily basis. The good news is that value is the most important variable when it comes down to your earning power. Companies don't mind paying a little bit more for a person who has a strong brand, because they trust that that person can deliver value. When high value has been placed on a product, service, or person, people will pay top dollar to get it. You can buy a steak for $5 or $50 depending on the brand of the restaurant. Consumers don't mind paying money for a product, service, or an employee who has a perceived high market value. Value is the determining factor in the brand.

Our personal brand is based on how we look, act, talk, and how we impact people, organizations and situations. We all have a brand in our homes, companies, neighborhoods, volunteer organizations and churches. Everywhere we go we start developing a brand the moment we arrive. The stronger our personal brand is, the more value we possess. Maybe you had a strong brand at some point and did something to weaken it. You may have weakened it to the point that you have lost confidence in yourself. Your quality of life is dependent on how strong your personal brand is. I have great news for you.... You are in total control of your personal brand and the improvement of it. Work on your brand every day and if it has been weakened, get right back to work and strengthen it. Your brand is the most important thing you possess.

You can't out-produce your self image.

– *Walter Bond*

CHAPTER EIGHT

The Man In The Mirror

Do you want to know the real reason people fall victim to the corporate *comfort zone*? Do you want to know what could be holding you back from increasing your income? The answer to the reason people settle for less in their lives is simple: **A person doesn't settle until they believe they are getting what they truly deserve out of life.** Your life is where it is because this is how you see yourself. As a man thinks, so is he. I am convinced that being successful and prospering can be easy, if you grasp this one simple principle. You will become exactly who you think you are.

A person's success is all about their self-image. If what you believe about yourself determines your success, then ask yourself, "What do I believe about myself?" Your self-image permeates every aspect of your life. Every decision you make you consult your self-image before making a final decision. In other words, with me being who I am, can I live with this? This question is buried deep in our subconscious mind. How you dress in the morning, with whom you interact, and how you interact with people, your self-image frames every aspect of your life. When I see a person struggle with life and quit, the question in my mind is this: *What happened to their self-image?* We all face struggles from time to time, it's a part of life that doesn't discriminate. *"But"* if your self-image is far beneath your potential--struggling becomes a lifestyle and you will settle for less.

What kind of lifestyle do you see yourself living? Do you see yourself as an executive type? Can you see yourself with a successful and attractive spouse? What you really believe about yourself is where you will ultimately end up in life. It will be what you settle for. You won't settle until you believe you are getting what you deserve. It doesn't really matter how big or small your vision is. You will become what you believe about yourself. I don't believe a person can ever settle for less than what they think they deserve. If you want your life to change, you must first change your self-image. The litmus test for self-image is an exercise in exposure. I challenge you to walk into a local country club. Why not? It's free! After the experience ask yourself. How did it make me feel? Can I really see myself as a member? Go and test drive a luxury car. Can you see yourself in it? The next time you have a free Saturday, go on a luxury home tour and keep looking at different sized homes and don't stop until you can no longer see yourself living in the houses you visit. If you can't see yourself living in it, that will give you a clue as to the limits of your self-image.

Our self-image begins to be formed the day we are born. It is crafted by our environment, culture, experiences, and relationships. Your self-image right now is a culmination of every day you have been alive. Your self-image is the sum total of every thought you've had about yourself and every word people have spoken to you. I want you to be in a position to maximize your skills and potential out of life. You can't out produce your own self-image. That's impossible. It is amazing that our own self-image can be lower than what others perceive of us and it also can be much higher. You should always be president of your own personal fan club. We should always think highly of ourselves (not too high, though). I have learned that confidence is arrogance under control. Arrogance is another form of poor self-image, believe it or not there is a direct correlation with arrogance to low self-esteem and low self-image.

Have you ever seen someone consistently date a person who doesn't seem to measure up to the kind of person you think they can attract? Have you ever seen someone work at a job or live in a condition that you thought they were better than? This dynamic confused me for years until I reached a certain level of maturity. I know people who are very dear to me who settle for less in their relationships, careers, living conditions, and in almost everything. It doesn't matter at all what you think they should have. What matters most is what *they* think they should have. What do you think you should have out of life? You see, people try to save their loved ones from dysfunctional relationships all the time. Just about the time you pry the person from one dysfunctional relationship, a new one pops up, and that relationship is worse than the previous one. Your focus shouldn't be on making sure your friend or loved one breaks up with their current suitor, because they'll only run to another as fast as you turn your head. If you want to really help them, help them improve their self-image. I promise you these poor relationships will disappear overnight once a person improves their self-image.

I think we all should make it a habit of helping boost the self-image of everyone we know and those we meet. You can become an instant star by committing to boost people's self-image. Why? Because it is the right thing to do. We have enough people polluting the planet with negativity and criticism. Give everyone you meet a boost by giving them a compliment when you see them—"nice smile", "your kids are well-behaved", "nice car", "you are so thoughtful." On the golf course it is customary to repair your divot (damaged soil) plus one more to keep the greens looking good. If you ever find yourself saying or doing anything to divot someone's self-image, remember it needs to be repaired. You can normally do this with a quick apology, You can also try to repair a divot that someone else may have caused whenever you encounter someone.

Before we can address the improvement of your self-image, we need to first walk down memory lane and understand how your self-image was formed. Research tells us that a personality and self-image is formed by the time a child is eight years of age. If your self-image has been formed by your environment, culture, and past experiences, this can give you some valuable insight into your personality today. I think the most powerful dynamic in developing a person's self-image is how that person has been nurtured, disciplined, and spoken to, early in life. If a child has been spoken well of, they have a much better chance of developing a healthy self-image. If a child is criticized early in life or abandoned, their self-image has probably been damaged before they even understand what self-image is and they can be very insecure and, in some cases, emotionally crippled. It is imperative that you always speak well of your own children and of children, in general. You want your child to have a healthy self-image. I have made it a habit to speak well of my children on a daily basis because their self-image will drive their behavior and their expectations out of life. The most critical element to my job as a parent is to help develop my children's self-image. If you have children, you should take responsibility of helping them form their self-image by what you say to them, showing enthusiasm for their successes, and giving encouragement and support when they struggle. You can build or destroy a child's self image by merely speaking the wrong words to them at the wrong time and in the wrong tone. I have not met a perfect family yet, so be courageous and honest about your background because it contains powerful information that can be the key to understanding your own self-image. There is even research that reveals the different dynamics of a child relative to their birth order. You may be the youngest child in your family--they tend to be fun-loving, comedians, best athletes or sometimes the weakest link. Middle children can be good referees obsessed with fairness, *"but"* they like to argue and stir things up. The oldest child can be more conservative and not so aggressive. There are so many variables that helped to form your self-image. It would take some thought to sort it all out, *"but"* it would be worth it.

There are some simple keys that can improve a person's self-image. These steps are good for everyone because we all can use a boost. *"But"* first of all, let's look at some characteristics of poor self-image. A person with a poor self-image can operate at two extremes: they tend to be very critical of themselves and others, they lack confidence and live in fear, *"but"*, as I mentioned earlier, someone with a poor self-image can also exhibit arrogant behavior. This show of arrogance is meant to camouflage a poor self-image *"but"* it is hard work to keep everything together. The show is to convince everyone that their self-image is strong, *"but"* the more they act it out the more they convince us otherwise. Trust me on this one! After an eight-year professional basketball career, I have seen both extremes. A consistent show of arrogance and bragging is a red flag for a poor self-image.

There are four keys to building your self-image

I. Think and speak well of yourself.

The key ingredient for improving your self-image is to genuinely think and speak well of yourself. It is so common to hear people bash themselves, as if it is okay. If you take offense when people speak poorly of you, why would you speak poorly of yourself? Have you ever heard someone call themself stupid, lazy or ugly? We see others who may not say an unkind word about themselves *"but"* their lifestyles are abusive. Remember a person's actions tell you the real story. You can't have a good self-image and then have a lifestyle with self-destructive behavior. I have met people who really don't love themselves, basically because no one has ever expressed love to them. Think well and speak well of yourself at all times. Love yourself at all times. If you don't, you can never receive love from anyone else. When a person tries to love you, you will reject it because you wouldn't think you deserve it. If your self-image is what it should be, you expect people to love you because you are lovable. Discipline your mind to always think well and speak well of yourself and others, and expect to hear complements accordingly.

II. Surround yourself with advocates.

Always surround yourself with people who are **advocates**— those who allow you to be yourself and support you, no matter what. This planet is full of actors. We have Emmy and Oscar winners everywhere who will never set foot on the big screen. It is hard work being on stage all of the time trying to convince people that you are someone you really aren't. There is nothing wrong with you that you should try to be someone other than yourself.

The worst travesty to a human life is for someone to become an actor in life; and thus, never become really who they are. It is so refreshing and liberating to be around people who believe in you, and allow you to be less than perfect. We are often afraid to share our inner struggles and emotions because we are afraid of what others will think of us once we share. You don't have true relationships until you can be transparent about yourself in a safe environment. Don't stop until you find these kinds of people, we all need advocates. A real advocate believes in you even when your imperfections are made public.

III. Spend Time with Catalysts.

Get around **catalysts,** which is a group of people who push you. Sometimes if you spend too much time with advocates you get mushy and soft and listen to "We are the world" songs all day. Don't ever forget that if there is no pain, there is no gain. I have a few advocates I lean on, *"but"* I joined a country club and love to do high-end networking because I love to be around catalysts, because they push me. I don't need to get intimate with this group; that is not why they are in my life. My advocates give me all the TLC I need. A catalyst's job is to push you. Find a group of people who have achieved a high level of success, hopefully a higher level of success than you. This can cover any area of your life: career, marriage, physical fitness, or spiritual life. Their influence will start to affect your confidence, and ultimately, your self-image. You will begin to see how much you have in common with them and this will help you to see yourself differently. Before you know it, you will learn that you can play at a higher level than before, thus creating a great boost to your self-image. Sometimes you need a hug from your advocates, *"but"* sometimes you just need a push from your catalysts. These two different groups help you to build and strengthen your self-image.

I must warn you of a third group of people to stay away from. **Haters!** Whatever you do, stay away from negative or jealous people. Negative people have a poor self-image and aren't equipped to help you build your self-image. Depending on how strong your self-image is, you may be able to stomach the conversation long enough to help boost their self-image. However, their influence is like kryptonite. Their influence will weigh you down and cause you to digress. Either way, please be mindful of how much time you invest with haters. Trust me on this one, it is not worth the investment in time.

IV. Look in the mirror and smile.

This key is the easiest one--just look in the mirror and smile. If a smile creates good will for other people you encounter, how much more will it bring satisfaction to you? Look in that mirror once a day and just smile. When you smile your mind must think happy thoughts. Look in the mirror and smile, and smile everywhere you go. I recently had a person ask me why do I smile so much? My thought was, *Why do you smile so little?*

When you have a good self-image you will hold out until life gives you what you deserve. Remember a person won't settle until they are getting what they think they deserve. I have learned through my experience that professional athletes hold out on their contracts all of the time. Fans complain and the media have a field day on their behalf and call them greedy. In some cases that is exactly what they are, *"but"* for the sake of this conversation, let's call them "convinced." Let's not miss the real nugget of wisdom here. Society misses the lesson being taught by a premier athlete.

We all can learn something from this. Now, I do believe that if you sign a contract you should honor the contract, *"but"* when an athlete holds out, this athlete is thoroughly convinced that he or she is worth more money and is willing to take a stand to get it. You know what, sometimes this strategy works because their confidence can convince everyone they are worth the amount they seek. It takes courage to take a stand and demand more out of life or your situation.

What stand have you made lately based on your self-image? Do you just settle for what your company says you're worth? What do you think you are worth? What value a person really places on themselves is clearly indicated by what salary they accept. A salary is something you receive, accept, or reject. There is a huge difference between the three. You can receive a salary and not accept it as your true value, you can accept a salary and receive it as your true value, or you can reject it all together and look until you receive a salary that you feel is in line with your true value. I recognize that we can accept a salary and not receive it as our true value, because we do have to start somewhere. My point is this: I believe when a person hits the *comfort zone* in the corporate world they are convinced they are being paid what they are really worth and their paycheck reflects their self-image. What salary do you currently receive? Have you accepted it as your true value? Does your self-image tell you that you are a $45,000 $50,000 or $100,000 person? You get to choose. Don't ever let anyone decide this for you, take control of this yourself. When a person's self-image is healthy, they will make a stand in their relationships too. They are comfortable being by themselves until they meet someone who meets their standards. You see, the key to helping someone achieve greatness is to nurture their self-image. My motivational programs are no good if I can't convince people they are worth more than they are currently receiving out of life. If I can't lift a person's self-image, I can't motivate them.

My own self-image has been tested. I can remember after I retired from professional basketball and put my resume together, I had very successful interviews *"but"* every job offer that came back was entry-level. I was thirty-years-old and I understood what these companies were thinking: *His resume was the same as a college graduate.* I had no work experience; therefore they saw me as entry-level. I knew I was much more valuable than they gave me credit for and it was very frustrating for me. Begrudgingly, I took an entry-level job as a job recruiter because this is what the marketplace said I was worth. I worked there for less than two months until I couldn't take it anymore. My self-image told me I was much more valuable than this job paid. One Friday evening after two months of work, I said to my wife, "I can't go back." I believed I was more valuable and I couldn't handle staying with a company that didn't reward me according to my true value. I worked hard while I was there *"but"* I just couldn't stay any longer. My self-image allowed me to make a stand for myself and my family.

That weekend we decided to found Walter Bond Seminars, and in less than five years we had more than replaced our NBA income in business, we doubled it. Your self-image will not allow you to accept anything that is far below your own perceived value. In this case my self-image helped me. I have also experienced the opposite. When I first started speaking I was terrified to speak in front of a corporate audience, so I would speak only to youth. I didn't believe I had a message to share with an adult audience. Why would a room full of executives listen to me? That was because of a poor self-image. The more I spoke, the more confident I became and that alone helped me to change my self-image as a speaker. This changed our business, changed our revenue, and changed our life. You won't settle in life until you believe you're getting what you deserve out of life. "***But***' my self-image is fine and it doesn't have anything to do with my lifestyle." ***ALL BUTS STINK!*** Your self-image *is* your lifestyle.

Introducing public seminars.

Visit us at

www.walterbondseminars.com

to find out schedule information